LV
LVI

ViVa

THE CUMMINGS TYPESCRIPT EDITIONS

*This series of the published and unpublished writings
of E.E.Cummings is based upon the author's typed and
autographed manuscripts in The Houghton Library,
Harvard University; the Clifton Waller Barrett Library,
University of Virginia; The University of Texas
Humanities Research Center; and The Beinecke Rare
Book and Manuscript Library, Yale University. The
cooperation and assistance of these institutions and
their librarians, curators, and staffs are hereby gratefully
acknowledged.*

*It is the aim of The Cummings Typescript Editions
to present the texts of the poet's works exactly as he
created them, in versions that are faithful to the letter as
well as the spirit of his originals. This does not present
any difficulties with reference to his plays, essays, letters,
and narrative prose. However, as Cummings himself
observed, it is impossible "to retranslate [his] poems [and
poetic prose] out of typewriter language into linotype-ese"
without distorting the spatial values of the works
themselves. The "typewriter language" of the poems and
poetic prose has therefore been retained. These works
have been prepared for publication by George James
Firmage, the editor of the series.*

E.E.Cummings

Edited, with an Afterword, by
George James Firmage

Liveright
NEW YORK

Published simultaneously in Canada
by George J. McLeod Limited, Toronto.
Printed in the United States of America.

FIRST EDITION

ALL RIGHTS RESERVED

Library of Congress Cataloging in Publication Data

Cummings, Edward Estlin, 1894–1962.
   W / E. E. Cummings.
   Title printed as overlapping V's.
   I. Firmage, George James. II. Title. III. Title: VV
PS3505.U334W2   1979   811'.5'2   79–4212
ISBN 0–87140–636–5
ISBN 0–87140–125–8 pbk.

1 2 3 4 5 6 7 8 9 0

ViVa

```
    ,mean-
hum
a)now

(nit
y unb
uria

ble fore(hurry
into
heads are
legs think wrists

argue)short(eyes do
bang hands angle
scoot bulbs marry a become)
ened
(to is

see!so
long door
golf slam bridge train shriek
chewing whistles hugest
to
morrow from smiles sin

k
ingly ele
vator glide pinn
)pu(
acle to

rubber)tres(plants how grin
ho)cen(tel
und
ead the

not stroll
living spawn imitate)ce(re
peat

credo fais do
do neighbours re babies
                        while;
```

oil tel duh woil doi sez
dooyuh unnurs tanmih eesez pullih nizmus tash,oi
dough un giv uh shid oi sez. Tom
oidoughwuntuh doot,butoiguttuh
braikyooz,datswut eesez tuhmih.   (Nowoi askyuh
woodundat maik yurarstoin
green? Oilsaisough.)—Hool
spairuh luckih? Thangzkeed. Mairsee.
Muh jax awl gawn. Fur Croi saik
ainnoughbudih gutnutntuhplai?
                HAI

yoozwidduhpoimnuntwaiv un duhyookuhsumpnruddur
givusuhtoonunduhphugnting

the surely

Cued
motif smites truly to Beautifully
retire through its english

the Forwardflung backwardSpinning hoop returns fasterishly
whipped the top leaps bounding upon other tops to caroming
off persist displacing Its own and their Lives who
grow slowly and first into different deaths

Concentric geometries of transparency slightly
joggled sink through algebras of proud

inwardlyness to collide spirally with iron arithmethics
and mesh witH
Which when both

march outward into the freezing fire of Thickness)points

uPDownwardishly
find everywheres noisecoloured
curvecorners gush silently perpetuating solids(More
fluid Than gas

there are 6 doors.
Next door(but
four)gentlemen are trinightly entertained by a whore
who Talks in the daytime,when who

is asleep with only several
faces and a multitude of chins:next door
but three dwells;a(ghost)Who
screams Faintly always

who Is bluish;next
Door but two occupy a man
and his wife:Both very young noisily
who kiss throw silently things

Each at other(if not
quarrelling in a luxury of telescoped
languages)she smokes three
castles He looks jewish

,next door but One
a on Dirty bed Mangy from person Porous
sits years its of self fee(bly
Perpetually coughing And thickly spi)tting

But next door nobody
seems to live at present(l'on
parle de repapering;i
don't think so.maybe:somebody?)or,bedbugs

myself,walking in Dragon st
one fine August
night,i just
happened to meet

"how do you do" she smiling
said "thought you
were earning your living
or probably dead"

so Jones was murdered by
a man named Smith and
we sailed on the
Leviathan

but mr can you maybe listen there's
me &
some people
and others please
don't
confuse.Some

people

's future is toothsome like
(they got
pockets full may take a littl
e nibble now And then
bite)candy

others
fly,their;puLLing:bright
futures
against the deep sky in

May mine's tou
ching this crump
led cap mumble some
thing to oh no
body will
(can you give
a)listen to
who may

you

be
any
how?
down
to
smoking
found
Butts

Space being(don't forget to remember)Curved
(and that reminds me who said o yes Frost
Something there is which isn't fond of walls)

an electromagnetic(now I've lost
the)Einstein expanded Newton's law preserved
conTinuum(but we read that beFore)

of Course life being just a Reflex you
know since Everything is Relative or

to sum it All Up god being Dead(not to

mention inTerred)
                LONG LIVE that Upwardlooking
Serene Illustrious and Beatific
Lord of Creation,MAN:
                at a least crooking
of Whose compassionate digit,earth's most terrific

quadruped swoons into billiardBalls!

VIII

(one fine day)

let's take the train
for because dear

whispered again
in never's ear
(i'm tho thcared

giggling lithped now
we muthn't pleathe
don't as pop weird
up her hot ow

you hurt tho nithe
steered his big was)
thither to thence
swore many a vow
but both made sense

in when's haymow
with young fore'er
(oh & by the way
asked sis breath
of brud breathe
how is aunt death

did always teethe

y is a WELL KNOWN ATHLETE'S BRIDE

(lullaby)
& z

=an infrafairy of floating
ultrawrists who
lullabylullaby

(I could have been
You,You
might have been I)
                    "?" quoth the

front;and there was yz
SHOT AND KILLED her
(in his arms)Self

                    & Him
self in the hoe tell days are

teased:

        let(however)us
Walk very (therefore and)softly among one's own
memory(but)along perhaps the
By invisibilities spattered(or if

it may be socalled)memory
Of(without more ado about less
than nothing)

                2 boston
Dolls;found
with
Holes in each other

's lullaby and
other lulla wise by UnBroken
LULLAlullabyBY

            the She-in-him with
the He-in-her(&

both all hopped
            up)prettily
then which did
lie
Down,honestly

now who go(BANG(BANG

          thethe
the pink

Tartskids with
thecas-tanets
in5/4; Time

          chick.chick
but:that Mat isse like

-with-the-chinese-eyebrowsMan
gave me,A,

(peach
      a soft eyes syriansing asong tohim self
all

about the desertbyIts elf
                          while) nextto
Mesmoked eleven camels
                    !

and i got a Bad almond
chick.
      thepinkisht artskiDs...

      with thema Tiss eeyeb Rowspeach es
a soft desert smoked bad me whilepin Kishcam elscasta;netsits
Elf
   allaBout .

          (chic)
                -kchi

cK,

a
 mong crum
        bling people(a
long ruined streets
hither and)softly

thither between(tumb
ling)
      houses(as
the kno

wing spirit prowls,its
nose winces
before a dissonance of

Rish and Foses)
            until
                (finding one's self
at some distance from the
crooked town)a

harbour fools the sea(
while
      emanating the triple
starred

Hotel du Golf...that notable structure
or ideal edifice...situated or established
...far from the noise of waters
)one's

eye perceives
              (as the ego approaches)
painfully sterilized contours;
within

which
"ladies&gentlemen"
—under

glass—
are:
asking.

?each
oth?
er

rub,
!berq;
:uestions

poor But TerFLY

went(flesh is grass)
from Troy,

n.y.
the way of(all
flesh is grass)with one "Paul"

a harvard boy
alas!
(who simply wor
shipped her)who

after not coming once in seven years expl0
ded like a toy eloping to Ire(land must be
heav

en
FoR

my

motH)with a grass wid
OW

er who smelt rath
er like her fath
er who smelt rath

er(Er
camef
romth
AIR

remarked Robinson Jefferson

to Injustice Taughed
your story is so interested

but you make me laft
welates Wouldwoe Washington
to Lydia E. McKinley

when Buch tooked out his C.O.D.
Abe tucks it up back inley
clamored Clever Rusefelt
to Theodore Odysseus Graren't

we couldn't free the negro
because he ant
but Coolitch wiped his valley forge

with Sitting Bull's T.P.
and the duckbilled platitude lays & lays

and Lays aytash unee

what time is it i wonder never mind
consider rather heavenly things and but
the stars for instance everything is planned
next to that patch of darkness there's a what
is it oh yes chair but not Cassiopeia's

might those be stockings dribbling from the table
all which seemed sweet deep and inexplicable
not being dollars toenails or ideas
thoroughly 's stolen(somewhere between

our unlighted hearts lust lurks
slovenly and homeless and when
a kiss departs our lips are made of thing

in beginning corners dawn smirks

and there's the moon,thinner than a watchspring

well)here's looking at ourselves

two solids in(all
one it)
solution(of
course you must shake well)

indolently dreaming puzzling

over that one
oh just thinking it over
(at that just supposing
we had met and just
but you know

supposing we

just had let it go at
that)that
seems important doesn't
it and
doesn't that seem
puzzling but we both might have found the solution

of that in

the importance of the
fact that(in spite of the fact
that i and that
you had carefully
ourselves decided what this cathedral ought to

look like)it doesn't look

at
all like what you
and what i(of course)
carefully had decided oh

no(but

        tell me not how electricity or
god was invented but
        why(captured by a
policeman's majestic and buried eye)

the almost large he-
        shaped object vomits cleverly
against a quai wall almost spray
        -ing threecoloured puke over

        this younger than
i am newspaper guy who refused
        to shake hands with
ludendorff and your humble moving through the

gloominess of(try to
        imagine)whispering
of a named
        Krassin

XVII

FULL SPEED ASTERN)

m

 usil(age)ini
sticks
tuh de mans

l

(hutch)hutchinson says sweet guinea
pigs do it buy uh cupl un
wait

k

(relijinisde)o(peemuvdepipl)
marx okays jippymugun
roomur

j

 e(wut)
hova
in big cumbine wid

i

(chek
undublchek)
babbitt

(GOD SAVE THE UNCOMMONWEALTH OF HUMANUSETTS

"Gay" is the captivating cognomen of a Young Woman of cambridge,mass.
to whom nobody seems to have mentioned ye olde freudian wish;
when i contemplate her uneyes safely ensconced in thick glass
you try if we are a gentleman not to think of(sh)

the world renowned investigator of paper sailors—argonauta argo
harmoniously being with his probably most brilliant pupil mated,
let us not deem it miraculous if their(so to speak)offspring has that largo
appearance of somebody who was hectocotyliferously propagated

when Miss G touched n.y. our skeleton stepped from his cupboard
gallantly offering to demonstrate the biggest best busiest city
and presently found himself rattling for that well known suburb
the bronx(enlivening an otherwise dead silence with harmless quips,out of Briggs by
                                                                              Kitty)

arriving in an exhausted condition,i purchased two bags of lukewarm peanuts
with the dime which her mama had generously provided(despite courteous protestations)
and offering Miss Gay one(which she politely refused)set out gaily for the hyenas
suppressing my frank qualms in deference to her not inobvious perturbations

unhappily,the denizens of the zoo were that day inclined to be uncouthly erotic
more particularly the primates—from which with dignity square feet turned abruptly
                                                                     Miss Gay away:
"on the whole"(if you will permit a metaphor savouring slightly of the demotic)
Miss Gay had nothing to say to the animals and the animals had nothing to say to Miss
                                                                                  Gay

during our return voyage,my pensive companion dimly remarked something about "*stuffed
fauna*" being "very interesting"...we also discussed the possibility of rain...
in distant proximity to a Y.W.c.a. she suddenly luffed
—thanking me;and(stating that she hoped we might "meet again

sometime")vanished,gunwale awash.   I thereupon loosened my collar
and dove for the nearest 1;surreptitiously cogitating
the dictum of a new england sculptor(well on in life)re the helen moller
dancers,whom he considered "elevating—that is,if dancing CAN be elevating"

Miss(believe it or)Gay is a certain Young Woman unacquainted with the libido
and pursuing a course of instruction at radcliffe college,cambridge,mass.
i try if you are a gentleman not to sense something un poco putrido
when we contemplate her uneyes safely ensconced in thick glass

XIX

i will cultivate within
me scrupulously the Inimitable which
is loneliness,these unique dreams
never shall soil their raiment

with phenomena:such
being a conduct worthy of

more ponderous
wishes or
hopes less
tall than mine"(opening the windows)

"and there is a philosophy" strictly at
which instant(leaped
into the

street)this deep immediate mask and
expressing "as for myself,because i
am slender and fragile
i borrow contact from that you and from

this you sensations,imitating a few fatally

exquisite"(pulling Its shawl carefully around
it)"things i mean the
Rain is no respecter of persons
the snow doesn't give a soft white
damn Whom it touches

but granted that it's nothing paradoxically enough beyond mere personal

pride which tends to compel me to decline to admit i've died)
seeing your bald intellect collywobbling on its feeble stem is

believing science=$(2b)^{-n}$ herr professor m

helves surling out of eakspeasies per(reel)hapsingly
proregress heandshe-ingly people
trickle curselaughgroping shrieks bubble
squirmwrithed staggerful unstrolls collaps ingly
flash a of-faceness stuck thumblike into pie
is traffic this recalls hat gestures bud
plumptumbling hand voices Eye Doangivuh sud-
denly immense impotantly Eye Doancare Eye
And How replies the upsquirtingly careens
the to collide flatfooting with Wushyuhname
a girl-flops to the Geddup curb leans
carefully spewing into her own Shush Shame

as(out from behind Nowhere)creeps the deep thing
everybody sometimes calls morning

Lord John Unalive(having a fortune of fifteengrand
£
thanks to the socalled fact that maost faolks rally demannd canned
saounds)
gloats
upon the possession of quotes keltyer close
"&"

aureally(yawning while all the dominoes)fall:down;in,rows

buncha hardboil guys frum duh A.C. fulla
hooch kiddin eachudder bout duh clap an
talkin big how dey could kill
sixereight cops—"I sidesteps im an draws
back huly jeezus"—an—"my
specialty is takin fellers' goils away
frum dem"—"somebody hung uh gun on
Marcus"—"duh Swede rolls down tree flights an Sam
begins boxin im on duh
koib"—you
know
alotta sweet bull like dat
                      ...suddenly
i feels so lonely fer duh good ole days we
spent in '18 kickin duh guts outa dem
doity frogeaters an humpin duh
swell janes on
duh boollevares an wid tears
streamin down my face i hauls
out uh glask an offers it tuh duh whole gang accrost
duh table—"fellers
have some
on
me"—dey was petrified.

De room swung roun an crawled up into
itself,
an awful big light squoits down my spine like
i was dead er sumpn:next i

knows me(er
somebody is sittin in uh green
field watchin four crows drop into
sunset,playin uh busted harmonica

XXIV

from the cognoscenti

bingbongwhom chewchoo
laugh dingle nails personally
bung loamhome picpac
obviously scratches tomorrowlobs

wholeagainst you gringlehow
exudes thursday fasters
by button of whisper sum blinked
he belowtry eye nowbrow

sangsung née whitermuch grab
sicksilk soak sulksuck whim
poke if inch dimmer twist on
permament and slap tremendous

sorrydaze bog triperight
election who so thumb o'clock
asters miggle dim a ram
flat hombre sin bangaroom

slim guesser goose pin yessir wheel
no sendwisp ben jiffyclaus
bug fainarain wee celebate
amaranth clutch owch

so chuck slop hight evolute
my eerily oh gargle
to jip hug behemoth
truly pseudo yours podia

of radarw leschin

murderfully in midmost o.c.an

launch we a Hyperluxurious Supersieve
(which Ultima Thule Of Plumbing shall receive

the philophilic name S.S.VAN MERDE)

having first put right sleuthfully aboard
all to—mendaciously speaking—a man

wrongers who write what they are dine to live

XXVI

        oh1d song

you Know
a fly and
his reflection walking upon

a mirror this is
friday 1

what

3 a fly
&

her his Its image
strutting(very
jerkily)not toucH-

ing because separated by an impregnable

Because(amount of inter
-vening)anyway You
know Separated what
i Mean

        (oweld song by
        ;neither you nor i and

by the way)

        ,which is not fly

the first president to be loved by his
bitterest enemies" is dead

the only man woman or child who wrote
a simple declarative sentence with seven grammatical
errors "is dead"
beautiful Warren Gamaliel Harding
"is" dead
he's
"dead"
if he wouldn't have eaten them Yapanese Craps

somebody might hardly never not have been unsorry,perhaps

XXVIII

serene immediate silliest and whose
vast one function being to enter a Toy and
emerging(believably enlarged)make how
many stopped millions of female hard for their
millions of stopped male to look at(now
-fed infantile eyes drooling unmind
grim yessing childflesh perpetually acruise
and her quick way of slowly staring and such hair)
the Californian handpicked thrill mechanically
packed and released for all this very diminishing
vicarious ughhuh world(the pertly papped
muchmouthed)her way of beginningly finishing
(and such hair)the expensively democratic tyrannically
dumb

       Awake,chaos:we have napped.

XXIX

in a middle of a room
stands a suicide
sniffing a Paper rose
smiling to a self

"somewhere it is Spring and sometimes
people are in real:imagine
somewhere real flowers,but
I can't imagine real flowers for if I

could,they would somehow
not Be real"
(so he smiles
smiling)"but I will not

everywhere be real to
you in a moment"
The is blond
with small hands

"& everything is easier
than I had guessed everything would
be;even remembering the way who
looked at whom first,anyhow dancing"

(a moon swims out of a cloud
a clock strikes midnight
a finger pulls a trigger
a bird flies into a mirror)

i sing of Olaf glad and big
whose warmest heart recoiled at war:
a conscientious object-or

his wellbelovéd colonel(trig
westpointer most succinctly bred)
took erring Olaf soon in hand;
but—though an host of overjoyed
noncoms(first knocking on the head
him)do through icy waters roll
that helplessness which others stroke
with brushes recently employed
anent this muddy toiletbowl,
while kindred intellects evoke
allegiance per blunt instruments—
Olaf(being to all intents
a corpse and wanting any rag
upon what God unto him gave)
responds,without getting annoyed
"I will not kiss your fucking flag"

straightway the silver bird looked grave
(departing hurriedly to shave)

but—though all kinds of officers
(a yearning nation's blueeyed pride)
their passive prey did kick and curse
until for wear their clarion
voices and boots were much the worse,
and egged the firstclassprivates on
his rectum wickedly to tease
by means of skilfully applied
bayonets roasted hot with heat—
Olaf(upon what were once knees)
does almost ceaselessly repeat
"there is some shit I will not eat"

our president,being of which
assertions duly notified
threw the yellowsonofabitch
into a dungeon,where he died

Christ(of His mercy infinite)
i pray to see;and Olaf,too

preponderatingly because
unless statistics lie he was
more brave than me:more blond than you.

memory believes
fragrance of a town(whose
dormers choke
and snore the steeples writhe with

rain)faces(at windows do not
speak and are ghosts or
huddled in the darkness of
cafés people drink

smile if here there(like lopsided
imaginations)
filled with newly murdered
flowers whispering barns

bulge a tiniest street or
three contains these prettiest
deaths without effort while
hungering churches(topped

with effigies of crowing
gold)nuzzle against summer
thunder(together)smell only
such blue slender hands of god

Wing Wong,uninterred at twice
fortyeight,succeeded in producing

sixtyfour maxims

whose)centripetal wisdom in
thirtytwo seconds centrifugally
is refuted by these(

particularly belonging to
a
retired
general)sixteen years

of rapid
animal whose swir
-ling(not too frequently
)skirt exhumes(which
buries again quick-

ly its
self in)while
a transparent blouse
even recklessly
juggles the jouncing
fruit of eager bosoms"
                                    Wing

Wong

XXXIII

      innerly

UningstrolL
(stamens&pistil
            silent
A s   groupingThe
6around one
darks to 7th s
         o howpale)
bluedmufFletomben

        outerly

jeT
ting lip ssixs ting
sWervesca
rletlycaR v Ingharness
Of
curvish(

     ,males await she
patiently 1

)littlecrownGrave
whose whorlclown of spreadnessed bE
rich from-soft quits(now)ly
Comes;
:lush
ly-smootHdumb droopnew-gree

N.lyestmostsaresl e A v e S

don't cries to please my
mustn't broke)life Is
like that please stroke

for now stroke answers(but
now don't you're hurting o
Me please you're killing)death

is like now That please
squirtnowing for
o squirting we're replies(at

which now O fear turned o Now
handspring trans
forming it

self int
o eighteen)Don't
(for)Please(tnights,on whose for

eheads shone
eternal pleasedon't;
rising:from the Shall.

what is strictly fiercely and wholly dies
his impeccable feathered with green facts
preening solemnity ignoring,through
its indolent lascivious caring eyes

watches;truly,curvingly while reacts
(sharp now with blood now accurately wan)
keenly,to dreamings more than truth untrue,

the best mouth i have seen on any man—
a little fluttering,at the enchanted dike
of whose lean lips,hovers how slenderly
the illustrious unknown

                         (warily as
their master's spirit stooping,Crusoelike
examines fearingly and tenderly

a recent footprint in the sand of was)

sunset)edges become swiftly
corners(Besides
which,i note how
fatally toward

twilight the a little
tilted streets spill lazily
multitudes out of final

towers;captured:in
the narrow light

of

inverno)this
is the season of
crumbling & folding
hopes,hark;feet(fEEt
f-e-e-t-noWheregoingaLwaYS

                    XXXVII

              how
ses humble.

Over thin earths chatterish

strut cuddle & shrink:
as through immediately
yeswind-faces peer

skies;whiteLy
are which stumbling eyes which
why in(thundering)by
When eaten

spaces grouse rocket know
quite,

slightly or
how at the yearhour tree-
    spires shout appalling

              deathmoney into
                    spiralS
                            and
Now(comes

un,

    season of in:wardly
of him(every)

who does
(where)not move
;is

    .crowned the with shrill
Nonleaf daemons and large The downlife gods of
shut
)

n(o)w

    the
how
   dis(appeared cleverly)world

iS Slapped:with;liGhtninG
!

  at
which(sha)lpounceupcrackw(ill)jumps

of
   THuNdeRB
       loSSo!M iN
-visiblya mongban(gedfrag-
ment ssky?wha tm)eani ngl(essNessUn
rolli)ngl yS troll s(who leO v erd)oma insCol

Lide.!high
       n , o ; w :
             theraIncomIng

o all the roofs roar
         drownInsound(
&
(we(are like)dead
)Whoshout(Ghost)atOne(voiceless)O
ther or im)
   pos
   sib(ly as
   leep)
     But l!ook—
        s

   U

   n:starT birDs(lEAp)Openi ng
t hing ; s(
—sing
)all are aLl(cry alL See)o(ver All)Th(e grEEn

?eartH)N,ew

An(fragrance)Of

(Begins)
millions

Of Tints(and)
&
(grows)Slowly(slowly)Voyaging

tones intimate tumult
(Into)bangs
minds into
dream(An)quickly

Not

un deux trois
der
    die

Stood(apparition.)
WITH(THE ROUND AIR IS FILLED)OPENING

thou

     firsting a hugeness of twi
                         -light
pale
     beyond soft-
liness than dream more sing

(buoyant & who
silently shall to rea- disa)

ular,

     (ppear ah!Star
               whycol

our
   ed
shy lurch small invin

cible nod oc
cul
   t ke
ylike writhe of brea

          Thing

```
twi-
     is -Light bird
ful
-ly dar
kness eats

a distance a
c(h)luck
(1)ing of just bells (touch)ing
?mind

(moon begins The
)
now,est hills er dream;new
.oh if

        when:
&
a
nd O impercept i bl
```

structure,miraculous challenge,devout am

upward deep most invincible unthing
—stern sexual timelessness,outtowering
this noisy impotence of not and same

answer,beginning,ecstasy,to dare:
prouder than all mountains,more than all
oceans various
                and while everywhere
beneath thee and about thyself a small
hoping insect,humanity,achieves
(moult beyond difficult moult)amazing doom
who standest as thou hast stood and thou shalt stand.

Nor any dusk but kneelingly believes
thy secret and each morning stoops to blend

her star with what huge merciful forms presume

XLIII

if there are any heavens my mother will(all by herself)have
one. It will not be a pansy heaven nor
a fragile heaven of lilies-of-the-valley but
it will be a heaven of blackred roses

my father will be(deep like a rose
tall like a rose)

standing near my

swaying over her
(silent)
with eyes which are really petals and see

nothing with the face of a poet really which
is a flower and not a face with
hands
which whisper
This is my beloved my

                    (suddenly in sunlight
he will bow,

& the whole garden will bow)

i'd think "wonder

if" if
i were a
child "we can see a bat in this
twilight")
          there one is

look

how it goes   like   a dream

(and between houses,really a kind of
mouse)but he has little wings
and here's my
hotel this is the
door(opening it i

think things

which
were supposed to
be out of my
reach
      ,they are like
jam on the shelf everybody guessed

was too high)

look

    (it's back again   there   therehere
And)i say "won't you"(remembering)
knowing that you
are afraid "go first" of dreams and little

bats & mice(and

                you,
you say "let's" going in
"take
hands" smiling "coming up
these dark stairs.

you
in win
ter who sit
dying thinking
huddled behind dir
ty glass mind muddled
and cuddled by dreams(or some
times vacantly gazing through un
washed panes into a crisp todo of
murdering uncouth faces which pass rap
idly with their breaths.)"people are walking deaths
in this season" think "finality lives up
on them a little more openly than usual
hither,thither who briskly busily carry the as
tonishing & spontaneous & difficult ugliness
of themselves with a more incisive simplicity a
more intensively brutal futility" And sit
huddling dumbly behind three or two partly tran
sparent panes which by some loveless trick sepa
rate one stilled unmoving mind from a hun
dred doomed hurrying brains(by twos
or threes which fiercely rapidly
pass with their breaths)in win
ter you think,die slow
ly "toc tic" as i
have seen trees(in
whose black bod
ies leaves
hide

XLVI

i met a man under the moon
on Sunday.
by way of saying
nothing he
smiled(but
just by the dirty collar of his

jacket were two glued uncarefully ears
in
that face of box of
skin lay eyes like
new tools)

whence i guessed that he also had climbed the pincian
to appreciate rome at nightfall;and because against this
wall his white sincere small
hands with their guessing fingers

did-not-move exquisitely
,like dead children
(if he had been playing a fiddle i had

been dancing:which is
why something about me reminded him of ourselves)

as Nobody came slowly over the town

when rain whom fear
not children but men
speaks(among leaves Easily
through voices womenlike telling

of death love earth dark)

and thousand
thrusts squirms stars
Trees,swift each with its

Own motion deeply to wickedly

comprehend the innocently Doomed
brief all which somewhere is

fragrantly,

arrive
        (when
Rain comes;
predicating forever,assuming
the laughter of afterwards—
i spirally understand

What

touching means
or What does a hand
with your hair
in my imagination

XLVIII

come a little further—why be afraid—
here's the earliest star(have you a wish?)
touch me,
before we perish
(believe that not anything which has ever been
invented can spoil this or this instant)
kiss me a little:
the air
darkens and is alive—
o live with me in the fewness of
these colours;
alone who slightly
always are beyond the reach of death

and the English

a light Out)
            & first of all foam

-like hair spatters creasing pillow
next everywhere hidinglyseek
no o god dear wait sh please o no O
3rd Findingest whispers understand
sobs bigly climb what(love being some-
thing possibly more intricate)i(breath
in breath)have nicknamed ecstasy and And

spills smile cheaply thick

—who therefore Thee(once and once only,Queen
among centuries universes between
Who out of deeplyness rose to undeath)

salute. and having worshipped for my doom
pass ignorantly into sleep's bright land

when hair falls off and eyes blur And
thighs forget(when clocks whisper
and night shouts)When minds
shrivel and hearts grow brittler every
Instant(when of a morning Memory stands,
with clumsily wilted fingers
emptying youth colour and what was
into a dirtied glass)Pills for Ills
(a recipe against Laughing Virginity Death)

then dearest the
way trees are Made leaves
open Clouds take sun mountains
stand And oceans do Not sleep matters
nothing;then(then the only hands so to speak are
they always which creep budgingly over some
numbered face capable of a largest nonglance the
least unsmile
or whatever weeds feel and fish think of)

a clown's smirk in the skull of a baboon
(where once good lips stalked or eyes firmly stirred)
my mirror gives me,on this afternoon;
i am a shape that can but eat and turd
ere with the dirt death shall him vastly gird,
a coward waiting clumsily to cease
whom every perfect thing meanwhile doth miss;
a hand's impression in an empty glove,
a soon forgotten tune,a house for lease.
I have never loved you dear as now i love

behold this fool who,in the month of June,
having of certain stars and planets heard,
rose very slowly in a tight balloon
until the smallening world became absurd;
him did an archer spy(whose aim had erred
never)and by that little trick or this
he shot the aeronaut down,into the abyss
—and wonderfully i fell through the green groove
of twilight,striking into many a piece.
I have never loved you dear as now i love

god's terrible face,brighter than a spoon,
collects the image of one fatal word;
so that my life(which liked the sun and the moon)
resembles something that has not occurred:
i am a birdcage without any bird,
a collar looking for a dog,a kiss
without lips;a prayer lacking any knees
but something beats within my shirt to prove
he is undead who,living,noone is.
I have never loved you dear as now i love.

Hell(by most humble me which shall increase)
open thy fire!for i have had some bliss
of one small lady upon earth above;
to whom i cry,remembering her face,
i have never loved you dear as now i love

it)It will it
Will come(we
being
unwound & gone into the ground)but

though

with wormS eyes
writhe amor(Though through

our hearts hugely squirm
roots)us
        ly;though
hither nosing lymoles cru.Ising

thither:t,ouch soft-ly me and eye(you
leSs

)ly(un
      der the mi
              croscopic world's

whens,wheels;wonders:
murders.cries:hopes;
houses,clouds.kisses,
lice;headaches:ifs.

)
 yet shall
our Not to
be

deciphered
selves

merely Continue to experience

a neverish subchemistry of
alWays
)fiercely live whom on

Large Darkness And The Middle Of
The
E

a
r
t
H

breathe with me this fear
(which beyond night shall go)
remembering only dare
(Wholly consider how

these immaculate thin
things half daemon half
tree among sunset dream
acute from root to leaf)

but should voices(whom lure
an eagerest strict flame)
demand the metaphor
of our projectile am

tell such to murder time
(forgetting what's to know
wholly imagining fire)
only consider How

if i love You
(thickness means
worlds inhabited by roamingly
stern bright faeries

if you love
me)distance is mind carefully
luminous with innumerable gnomes
Of complete dream

if we love each(shyly)
other,what clouds do or Silently
Flowers resembles beauty
less than our breathing

speaking of love(of
which Who knows the
meaning;or how dreaming
becomes

if your heart's mine)i
guess a grassblade
Thinks beyond or
around(as poems are

made)Our picking it. this
caress that laugh
both quickly signify
life's only half(through

deep weather then
or none let's feel
all)mind in mind flesh
In flesh succeeding disappear

lady will you come with me into
the extremely little house of
my mind. Clocks strike. The

moon's round,through the window

as you see and really i have no
servants. We could almost live

at the top of these stairs,there's a free
room. We almost could go(you
and i)into a together whitely big
there is but if so or so

slowly i opened the window a
most tinyness,the moon(with white wig
and polished buttons)would take you away

—and all the clocks would run down the next day.

somewhere i have never travelled,gladly beyond
any experience,your eyes have their silence:
in your most frail gesture are things which enclose me,
or which i cannot touch because they are too near

your slightest look easily will unclose me
though i have closed myself as fingers,
you open always petal by petal myself as Spring opens
(touching skilfully,mysteriously)her first rose

or if your wish be to close me,i and
my life will shut very beautifully,suddenly,
as when the heart of this flower imagines
the snow carefully everywhere descending;

nothing which we are to perceive in this world equals
the power of your intense fragility:whose texture
compels me with the colour of its countries,
rendering death and forever with each breathing

(i do not know what it is about you that closes
and opens;only something in me understands
the voice of your eyes is deeper than all roses)
nobody,not even the rain,has such small hands

LVIII

if there a flower(whom
i meet anywhere)
able to be and seem
so quite softly as your hair

what bird has perfect fear
(of suddenly me)like these
first deepest rare
quite who are your eyes

(shall any dream
come a more millionth mile
shyly to its doom
than you will smile)

LVIX

my darling since
you and
i are thoroughly haunted by
what neither is any
echo of dream nor
any flowering of any

echo(but the echo
of the flower of

Dreaming)somewhere behind us
always trying(or sometimes trying under
us)to is it
find somehow(but O gracefully)a
we,entirely whose least

breathing may surprise
ourselves
          —let's then
despise what is not courage my

darling(for only Nobody knows
where truth grows why
birds fly and
especially who the moon is.

because i love you)last night

clothed in sealace
appeared to me
your mind drifting
with chuckling rubbish
of pearl weed coral and stones;

lifted,and(before my
eyes sinking)inward,fled;softly
your face smile breasts gargled
by death:drowned only

again carefully through deepness to rise
these your wrists
thighs feet hands

poising
        to again utterly disappear;
rushing gently swiftly creeping
through my dreams last
night,all of your
body with its spirit floated
(clothed only in

the tide's acute weaving murmur

if you and i awakening

discover that(somehow
in the dark)this world has been
Picked,like a piece
of clover,from the green meadow of

time

lessness;quietly
                    turning
toward me the
guessable mirrors which your eyes are

You will communicate a little

more than twice all that
so
gently
while we were asleep while
we were each other disappeared:but i

slightly

smiling,
gradually shall reenter the

singular kingdom

(sleep)
        .while some
thing else
kisses busily
a
memory,which how exquisitely
flutters in

the cornerless tomorrow

item:is

       Clumsily with of
what manshaped shimpered how
                    girllike
laughtering blocks when

builds
its invisibly skil
ful toyTown
which upups to dowNdown
(and only where remembers

look,
      this was of a child
's shy foot among cool ferns

)
 therefore togethering our

wholly lives Givehurling
with your my most
:locking

        foreverfully

blend
    we a universe of gulls'
drift Of thickly
             starhums wherefore

& wormSmile eternal;quite
perhaps as sternly
much not life nor stop as
a tear is darker than a mile.

be unto love as rain is unto colour;create
me gradually(or as these emerging now
hills invent the air)
                        breathe simply my each how
my trembling where my still invisible when. Wait

if i am not heart,because at least i beat
—always think i am gone like a sun which must go
sometimes,to make an earth gladly seem firm for you:
remember(as those pearls more than surround this throat)

i wear your dearest fears beyond their ceaselessness

(nor has a syllable of the heart's eager dim
enormous language loss or gain from blame or praise)
but many a thought shall die which was not born of dream
while wings welcome the year and trees dance(and i guess

though wish and world go down,one poem yet shall swim

granted the all
                    saving our young kiss only
must unexist,solemnly and per rules
apparelling its soullessness by lonely
antics of ridiculous molecules)

nakedest(aiming for hugely the
ignorant most precise essential flame
never which waked)& perfectingly We

dive

        out of tinying time
                        (into supreme

Now:
    feeling memory shrink from such brief
selves as fiercely seek findingly new
textures of actual cool stupendous is

nor may truth opening encompass true)
while your contriving fate,my sharpening life

are(behind each no)touching every yes

but being not amazing:without love
separate,smileless—merely imagine your

sorrow a certain reckoning demands...

marvelling And what may have become of
with his gradual acute lusting glance
an alert clumsily foolishwise

(tracking the beast Tomorrow by her spoor)
over the earth wandering hunter whom you
knew once?

      what if(merely suppose)

mine should overhear and answer Who
with the useless flanks and cringing feet
is this(shivering pale naked very poor)
creature of shadow,that among first light

groping washes my nightmare from his eyes?

nothing is more exactly terrible than
to be alone in the house,with somebody and
with something)
                    You are gone.   there is laughter

and despair impersonates a street

i lean from the window,behold ghosts,
                                        a man
hugging a woman in a park.   Complete.

and slightly(why?or lest we understand)
slightly i am hearing somebody
coming up stairs,carefully
(carefully climbing carpeted flight after
carpeted flight.   in stillness,climbing
the carpeted stairs of terror)

and continually i am seeing something

inhaling gently a cigarette(in a mirror

put off your faces,Death:for day is over
(and such a day as must remember he
who watched unhands describe what mimicry,

with angry seasalt and indignant clover
marrying to themselves Life's animals)

but not darkness shall quite outmarch forever
—and i perceive,within transparent walls
how several smoothly gesturing stars are clever
to persuade even silence:therefore wonder

opens a gate;the prisoner dawn embraces

hugely some few most rare perfectly dear
(and worlds whirl beyond worlds:immortal yonder
collidingly absorbs eternal near)

day being come,Love,put on your faces

LXVIII

but if a living dance upon dead minds
why,it is love;but at the earliest spear
of sun perfectly should disappear
moon's utmost magic,or stones speak or one
name control more incredible splendor than
our merely universe,love's also there:
and being here imprisoned,tortured here
love everywhere exploding maims and blinds
(but surely does not forget,perish,sleep
cannot be photographed,measured;disdains
the trivial labelling of punctual brains...
—Who wields a poem huger than the grave?
from only Whom shall time no refuge keep
though all the weird worlds must be opened?
)Love

so standing,our eyes filled with wind,and the
whining rigging over us,i implore you to
notice how the keen ship lifts(skilfully
like some bird which is all birds but more fleet)
herself against the air—and whose do you
suppose possibly are certain hands,terse
and invisible,with large first new stars
knitting the structure of distinct sunset

driving white spikes of silence into joists
hewn from hugest colour
                         (and which night hoists
miraculously above the always
beyond such wheres and fears or any when
unwondering immense directionless
horizon)
          —do you perhaps know these workmen?

here is the ocean,this is moonlight:say
that both precisely beyond either were—
so in darkness ourselves go,mind in mind

which is the thrilling least of all(for love's
secret supremely clothes herself with day)

i mean,should any curious dawn discuss
our mingling spirits,you would disappear
unreally;as this planet(understand)

forgets the entire and perpetual sea

—but if yourself consider wonderful
that your(how luminous)life toward twilight will
dissolve reintegrate beckon through me,
i think it is less wonderful than this

only by you my heart always moves

AFTERWORD

by

George James Firmage

The final steps in *ViVa*'s progress to publication can be traced in an exchange of letters and cables between E. E. Cummings and S. A. Jacobs which are now in the Clifton Waller Barrett Library at the University of Virginia.[1] In the earliest of these, a letter dated July 4, 1930, the poet asked his "poem-printer" to "tell [Pascal] Covici [of Covici-Friede] to hurry the publication of [a book without a title and *CIOPW,* a selection of paintings and drawings in charcoal, ink, oils, pencil and watercolours]; for i've a bookofpoems almost ready for him(?)"

But the "bookofpoems" was still unfinished when, later that year, Cummings embarked for Europe to spend Christmas in Berlin, the first four months of the new year in Paris, and mid-May to mid-June on his now famous journey through Russia. However, writing from Paris on January 27, 1931, the poet notified Jacobs that "a few days ago I mailed you...the complete ms of 'viva'—seventy poems, with an index of firstlines (in case a question of order arose)." The typescript reached the printer sometime in March; and in late April, Jacobs wrote to say that Horace Liveright, rather than Covici, had agreed to publish *ViVa* on terms arranged by Cummings' literary agent in New York. The poet cabled on the fifth of May: "DOUBLY DELIGHTED AS LEAVE FOR MILLIONAIRISH MOSCOW THIS SATURDAY..."

By the end of July Cummings was back in the United States and in residence at the family farm in Silver Lake, New Hampshire. Here he proofread the galleys of his poems and began the arduous task of transcribing the journal he'd kept during his visit to Russia. Corrected proofs of *ViVa,* together with separate lists of errors and last minute alterations, continued to pass between the poet and his printer until the first week in September when final page proofs reached Silver Lake. Cummings acknowledged their arrival on the ninth of the month and assured Jacobs that "everyone (including myself) is captured per the titlepage, type, makeup, etc. To go into mourning for a moment: what about XXXII, line 13, [for] 'to' [read] 'too'; or XLIII, line 9, [for] 'silent)' [read] '(silent)' in yellow proof?" It was, however, too late. The book as published by Liveright on October 16, 1931, contained not only the errors noted but more than a dozen additional mistakes.

The present edition of *ViVa* is based on the copy of the typescript Cummings sent to Jacobs which is now in The Houghton Library, Harvard University.[2] Unfortunately the manuscript is incomplete: four of the poems—LXVII to LXX—are missing. However, separate texts for two of the poems—LXIX and LXX—were found in The Houghton Collection;[3] and the text of a third—LXVII—was uncovered at The University of Texas Humanities Research Center, Austin.[4] These sets of galley proofs—two at The Houghton[5] and another at the University of Virginia[6]—as well as a final set of page proofs also at The Houghton[7] were consulted. All of the poet's final alteration and corrections have been adopted. A few misspellings of proper nouns have been silently corrected.

Notes

[1] All quotations from the Cummings-Jacobs correspondence are taken from the originals listed under Deposit 6246-a.

[2] bMs Am 1823.4 (25).

[3] bMs Am 1823.5 (320), 'so standing, our eyes filled with wind, and the'; bMs Am 1823.5 (120), 'here is the ocean, this is moonlight:say'.

[4] Ms (Cummings, EE) Works, 'put off your faces, Death:for day is over'.

[5] bMs Am 1823.4 (26) and bMs Am 1823.4 (27).

[6] Deposit 6246-a.

[7] bMs Am 1823.4 (28).